SCIFAIKUEST
August 2024

6	A Little Help, Please
10	Editorial
12	The John Gant Page
13	The John Granville Page
14	The Stephen C. Curro Page
15	The John Dromey Page
16	The David C. Kopaska-Merkel Page
17	The Yuliia Vereta Page
18	The Wendy Van Camp Page
19	The Roxanne Barbour Page
20	The Herb Kauderer Page
21	The H. T. Grossen Page
22	The N. E. Taylor Page
23	The Kate Lisinska Page
24	The Randall Andrews Page
25	Black and White Night by Gabriel Smithwilson
26	Scifaiku
33	Fairy with Wand by Denise Noe
34	Other Minimalist Forms
43	Robot Baldur by Denise Noe
44	Article: Headlines and Bullwhips by Robert E. Porter
49	Article: Kimo Word Pictures by Herb Kauderer
55	Head Held High by ARPY
56	Featured Poet: Tyler McIntosh
62	Interview: Tyler McIntosh
65	t.santitoro: my favorite poem

THE STAFF OF SCIFAIKUEST:
TERI SANTITORO, EDITOR

SCIFAIKUEST is published quarterly online and in print. The two editions are different.

Cover art "Moon Goddess" by Sandy DeLuca
Cover design by Laura Givens

Vol. XXII, No. 1   August 2024
Scifaikuest [ISSN 1558-9730] is published quarterly on the 1st day of February, May, August, and November in the United States of America by Hiraeth Publishing, P.O. Box 1248, Tularosa, NM 88352. Copyright 2024 by Hiraeth Publishing. All rights revert to authors and artists upon publication. Nothing may be reproduced in whole or in part without written permission from the authors and artists. Any similarity between places and persons mentioned in the fiction or semi-fiction and real places or persons living or dead is coincidental. Writers and artists guidelines are available online at https://www.hiraethsffh.com/scifaikuest.
Guidelines are also available upon request from Hiraeth Publishing, P.O. Box 1248, Tularosa, NM, 88352, if request is accompanied by a SASE #10 envelope with a first-class US stamp. Subscriptions: $28 for one year [4 issues], $44 for two years [8 issues]. Single copies $9.00 postage paid in the United States. Subscriptions to Canada: $33 for one year, $51 for two years. Single copies $11.00 postage paid to Canada. U.S. and Canadian subscribers remit in U.S. funds. All other countries inquire about rates.

What???
No subscription to
Scifaikuest??

We can fix that . . .

https://www.hiraethsffh.com/product-page/scifaikuest-1

Or get a sample back issue to check us out!

https://www.hiraethsffh.com/shop-1

And a subscription makes a great gift, for a holiday or any time of the year!

Minimalism:
A Handbook of Minimalist Genre Poetic Forms

This handbook contains articles about how to write various minimalist poetry forms such as scifaiku, senryu, sijo, haibun, empat perkataan, ghazals, cinquain, cherita, rengays, rengu, octains, tanka, threesomes, and many more. Each article is written by an expert in that particular poetry form.

Teri Santitoro, aka sakyu, who assembled this handbook, has been the editor of Scifaikuest since 2003.

https://www.hiraethsffh.com/product-page/minimalism-a-handbook-of-minimalist-genre-poetic-forms

A Little Help, Please

In the world of the small indie press we fight a never-ending battle for attention to our work, as writers and in publishing. Here's an example: big publishers [you know who they are] have gobs of $$$ that they can devote to advertising and marketing. Here at Hiraeth Publishing, our advertising budget consists of the deposits for whatever soda bottles and aluminum cans we can find alongside the highways. Anti-littering laws make our task even more difficult . . . ☺

That's where YOU come in. YOU are our best promoter. YOU are the one who can tell others about us. Just send 'em to our website, tell them about our store. That's all. Just that.

Of course, we don't mind if you talk us up. We're pretty good, you know. We have some award-winning and award-nominated writers and artists, plus other voices well-deserving to be heard [not everyone wins awards, right?] but our publications are read-worthy nevertheless.

That number once again is:
www.hiraethsffh.com

Friend us on Facebook at Hiraeth Publishing

Follow us on Twitter at @HiraethPublish1

SALE!!

There's a sale going on!! It's still going on!!

All the books you can order at 20% off the total! Woot!

Buy 1 book; buy 100 books! It's all the same discount. Use the code **BOOKS2024** when you check out.

Go to the Shop at <u>www.hiraethsffh.com</u> and make those selections now!

You'll be glad you did. So will we.

Aliens, Magic, and Monsters
By Lauren McBride

Fun to read. Fun to write. *Aliens, Magic, and Monsters* features poems set in the unlimited and imaginative realm of science fiction, fantasy, and horror. The poems were chosen to showcase over twenty poetic forms from acrostiku to zip, from strict rhyme to free verse, and much more in between. There are guidelines included on how to write each type of poem. Try a sci(na)ku. At only six words, it's sure to interest even the youngest readers.

Type: Juvenile and Young Adult Poetry Manual

Ordering links:
Print: https://www.hiraethsffh.com/product-page/aliens-magic-and-monsters-by-lauren-mcbride

ePub: https://www.hiraethsffh.com/product-page/aliens-magic-and-monsters-by-lauren-mcbride-2

PDF: https://www.hiraethsffh.com/product-page/aliens-magic-and-monsters-by-lauren-mcbride-1

Happy 22nd Anniversary, Readers!

From its inception more than two decades ago, I've had the pleasure, privilege and honor to serve as the editor of *Scifaikuest*.

Over the years, I've gotten to know many brilliant poets, artists and authors, from our newest contributors, to those who have stood with us from the beginning. But the one person who stands out the most, the one responsible for the awesome opportunity to be involved so thoroughly in the creation and continuation of *Scifaikuest,* is our managing editor, **Tyree Campbell**. To say that I'm grateful is just so inadequate. *Scifaikuest* and our family at Hiraeth Publishing have changed my life in uncountable ways, and I'm forever indebted to all of them, but especially to **Mr. Campbell**. Each anniversary, I recount in my mind how blessed I am to be part of this marvelous universe of publishing.

So. A toast from all of us here at *Scifaikuest,* wishing all of you, our Readers, another happy anniversary, and many more. Good health to all or, as **Mr. Campbell** would say, "*Slainte!*"

Scifaikuest now has it's own ISBN!!! Please inform your local book stores and library that they are now able to ORDER SCIFAIKUEST!!!

You can now find us at Hiraeth Books at:
https://www.hiraethsffh.com/home-1

If you don't have a subscription to our PRINT edition, they are available at:
https://www.hiraethsffh.com/product-page/scifaikuest

And, if you would like to join the select group of contributors by submitting your poetry, artwork or article, you can find our guidelines at:
https://www.hiraethsffh.com/scifaikuest
You can also read our ONLINE VERSION at:
https://www.hiraethsffh.com/scifaikuest-online

Pssst! Looking for something good to read?
You can get t.santitoro's newest novella, Those Who Die, at: THOSE WHO DIE by t. santitoro | Hiraeth Publishing (hiraethsffh.com)

You can also order **t.santitoro's** novella, *Adopted Child*, at: https://www.hiraethsffh.com/product-page/adopted-child-by-t-santitoro

You can also get a copy of her novelette, *The Legend of Trey Valentine*, at:
https://www.hiraethsffh.com/product-page/legend-of-trey-valentine-by-teri-santitoro

As always, a huge *Scifaikuest* Welcome to our newest contributors: **John Grey, Tyrean Martinson, Jacob R. Moses, H.V. Patterson** and **N.E. Taylor.**

PLEASE NOTE: *In the May 2024 PRINT issue, John J. Dunphy's work titled, "A Sestet", was actually a five-line minimal poem rather than a six-line sestet. My sincere apologies to Mr. Dunphy for mislabeling his poem!*

vacation on Croy
the aroma of kelp cakes
and tacky sunscreen
-sakyu-

The John Gant Page

Hues

chemicals in cones
rainbows dancing in my eyes
do we see the same

RNA

amino acids
dancing with their faded genes
what is the message

wonder

dragons and spaceships
fast flights of fun and fancy
modern myths alive

The John Granville Page

koan

solar wind
chimes
in a Dyson tree

Lost Generation

Lost Generation
found again
Tesla's cryogenics

accept no substitutes

your self-consciousness
a ship of Theseus
troubled immortality

The Stephen C. Curro Page

red dwarf sunrise
black moss
soft as silk

misty dawn...
at my touch the words
on the scroll glow

searing sun
knapping arrowheads
from dragon bone

desperate escape
into the river...
I wonder if T. rex can swim

The John Dromey Page

head spinning
so is planet
though not in sync

twice as sad now
and almost as lonely
me and my clone

humidifier
low-cost low-tech substitute
sweaty astronauts

The David C. Kopaska-Merkel Page

grib-tree nuts
snuggled up in our bed
motile seeds

under the mask
the senator's human head
99 to 1

the kid's
wishing on falling stars
Dad's coming home

leave the bar
at moonrise tonight
spare your friends

The Yuliia Vereta Page

bunch of navel-cords
in yesterdays' meatball soup
alien's cookbook

glitter on suckers
doing my best to adjust
still human inside

in the deep abyss
tentacles reach out to us
alien embrace

lips touch in the dark
alien love forbidden
interstellar hearts

The Wendy Van Camp Page

under the full moon
dual motherships arrive
lenticular clouds

tedious capture
as the crescent moon wanes
asteroid in tow

rivers shrink to sand
within eye of Sahara
losing Atlantis

The Roxanne Barbour Page

rising
from the lake
flowering offworld fish

lost expedition
found on Venus
devouring the planet

for trade
alien funeral urn
contents included

graveyards desecrated
bones removed
ground to dust by AIs

The Herb Kauderer Page

a transfer of certainty

far from the homeworld
unrelenting calendar
he curses tax day

someone's pet

animatronic
the artificial puppy
still misses his child

liminating weight

recreation stop
lunar ships depart lighter
from space casino

after the crash

rock paper scissors
loser unhooks his air tank
survivors roulette

The H. T. Grossen Page

MMO

lonely avatar
knight stands eternally still
his Player grew old

Fruit Salad on Venus

plantains and crushed mango
recipe from Mama's Earth
newly formed tropics

Navigator

blind pilots steer ships
detecting radiation waves
dragons in the stars

The N. E. Taylor Page

the cat's whiskers
glittering electrodes
now i understand

little robot
vacuum cleaner
my toes are not snacks

i know the names
of ghosts
old answering machine

summer forever yet
the grass is always greener
earthside

The Kate Lisinska Page

mountain wanderer
catching stars on the horizon
have to go back down

sunrise
chill wind comes
from an abandoned house

forest pond
starship's reflection
toads croaking

meteor rain
closer
than birthday candles

The Randall Andrews Page

stay-at-home swingers
no need to find new partners
shape-shifter romance

combustion coverage
prohibitively pricey
jetpack insurance

first opening night
Romeo and Juliet
time travel date night

Black and White Night
Gabriel Smithwilson

SCIFAIKU

cloud cover
Ursa Major
suddenly tailless

    John Grey

alien craft hover over lily pad
first contact
tongue of a frog

    John Grey

rogue planet
swinging round
to visit home

    Christina Sng

after it hit me
the aftereffects
of antigravity

    Christina Sng

Survivor

the last flesh
in this chromium jungle
all servos and steel

    Anthony Bernstein

Balance

hung in the balance
between the heavens and earth
are resting mothers

    Jacob R. Moses

thirty-second delivery
or you don't pay anything
hyperspace pizza

    Gabriel Smithwilson

ring around the collar
astronaut wears it proudly
Saturn souvenir

    Guy Belleranti

bouncing planetary tunes
transport me
takeoff

    Tyrean Martinson

dusk mingles light with dark
Drakkons and Humans
moonrise on Fayet

    Tyrean Martinson

warmth
we fear it
one sun becoming four

    Portia Rayshel

pink nectar
a soda replacement
home to lunar parasites

    Portia Rayshel

What's Out There

faith an abstract notion
realizing in the gamut of unknowns
God is a Cryptid

    Denise Hatfield

SENRYU

    cursed ...
    his delicate bones
    made of jade

        Deborah Karl-Brandt

    the chasm between us
    too vast to ponder
    morning on Mars

        Douglas J. Lanzo

    AI
    crosses a red line
    sending this senryu

        Douglas J. Lanzo

Bonnie and Clyde
erupt from foul crypt
rob blood banks

    Gary Davis

I know how you feel
the A.I. counselor said
with your fingertips

    John H. Dromey

hula dancer
radioactive grass skirt
toxic waist

    John H. Dromey

HORRORKU

abandoned psychiatric hospital
moving
Ouija board pointer

    Roxanne Barbour

online funeral
some sort of interference
moves through the pixels

    John Hawkhead

ghost train
lurking in the window
my evil twin

    John Hawkhead

spring breeze ...
the dropping sound of
a melting heart

    Deborah Karl-Brandt

now we know
mummy's curse is mold fungus
gift-wrapped death

    Gary Davis

The Boy Who Knew No Fear

amygdala misfire–
walking into hungry jaws
laughing at death

    H.V. Patterson

In Hungry Times

when the famine doesn't end
Mother's desperate hands reveal
you're not the favorite child

-H.V. Patterson

I'm food
on the prisoner's
plate

Barbara Anna Gaiardoni

at my doorstep
with a begging bowl
tattered flesh for clothes

the revenant, by Benjamin Whitney Norris

last night alone
chained to a stump
waiting for the parasites

last night alone, by Benjamin Whitney Norris

bald tire sandal
under my twenty-stone
slips from a high mountain path

avalanche, by Benjamin Whitney Norris

Fairy with Wand
Denise Noe

TANKA

embarrassment from
inappropriate contact
now using the space travelers'
guide to various
alien intimate zones

    Lauren McBride

in dancing unison
a million starry lights
aloft in alien skies
all aware
of our presence

    Richard E. Schell

ancient ruins
lost civilization
long abandoned
can we know
your long forgotten dreams

    Richard E. Schell

our robotic probes
scattered widely
across the galaxy
we found your world
but ours is long since passed

    Richard E. Schell

fearing contact
consequences unforeseen
questioning their intentions
we ask
can we trust our own

    Richard E. Schell

the greens attract
Herb Kauderer

golf course on Luna
built well before the resort
the fairway of dreams
delights a retiree
two thousand yards off the tee

starting over
Quillan Sprague

judgement of fire
a dead planet's smoking ruins
desolation's hush
reigns deep in the ocean's corpse
new weird life forms being born

OTHER FORMS (including: Sijo, Fibonacci, Cinquain, Minutes, Diminuendo, Ghazals, Threesomes, Brick, etc.)

SATURNE

socks

long hours

in space boots

o v e r w h e l m i n g

smell

Lauren McBride

soft

patter

on MarsDome

not a sand storm -

rain!

Lauren McBride

SEDOKA

non-negotiable -
non-interference
for peaceful explorers

except wherever
one sentient species
enslaves another

Lauren McBride

CRAPSEY CINQUAIN

Intertidal Zone

Four moons
loom silently
above the horizon
pulling the tide away, away,
away...

Robert P. Hansen

MINIMAL POEM

home alone
Denise Noe

home
alone
for a century
for a thousand years
rub oh! rub sweet human
set me free
this genie

CHERITA

Let's Do Lunch

I've eaten my fill

don't call it cannibalism
the most intimate kind of love

your memories flood my brain
we're young again, together
our whole lives ahead

David C. Kopaska-Merkel

FIBONACCI

scientists at work
by Denise Noe

space
ship
flying
galaxy
boldly traveling
on our scientific mission
learning, recording the secrets of our milky way

JOINED POEMS (incl. renku and sedoka, joined fib. Etc.,)

JOINED FIBONACCI

you
step
into
the greenhouse
where the flowers wait
and like previous visitors
you quickly become
enchanted
by their
scent
and
beauty
and you fall
in love with each bloom
and each bloom falls in love with you
and they hug you tight
bury you
then feed
on
you

--Guy Belleranti

HAIBUN and DRABBUN

HAIBUN

Farside Abbey
Banks Miller

We chose this place to pray and meditate, since calm comes here as nowhere else. The dust and stone of the lunar highlands are unstirred by wind or wave. Here reaches only the Sun's soft breath, fainter than the gentlest breeze's edge, and the subtle strains of space itself - stillness unequaled. These rocks have not been worn by wind or carved by rain since their molten birth eons ago.

The blazing fire of the long Lunar day, unfiltered by atmosphere, gives way to true night, with clearer stars than ever shine in airy skies. Here sunset is an instant; no twilight lingers, but full day becomes deep night in a heartbeat's space. And the silent mass of the Moon blocks out the radio clamor of Earth.

windless onyx skies
behind Luna's guard
true calm rests

The Primal Burn
Anthony Bernstein

Rage stands between reason and the primal burn, locked in futile combat with the land, sea and air. By fury's flaming sword, wielded with madness and grace, rage conjures a crimson gale to stain the hands of time, shreds the firmament to midnight confetti, drains our milky heavens starless.

Wielding sword of flame
rage storms the age of reason
to plant his red flag

Release havoc's ambassadors! Let them blast hemlock and shadows down the corridors of future history. Loose the architects of lunacy! Let them through wholesale slaughter to slather the globe with the shiney gore of multitudes, and none shall win the wounded day. No victorious army's, no grand military parades. No medals of honor nor heroes to decorate. No glory found here and only smoldering gray matter and mutual annihilation balance the world on a pin.

the hanging sword
the filament
cut

DRABBUN

"Untimely.'
Randall Andrews

It only took me six months to build the time machine, but two weeks after its completion, I still hadn't tested it. One nagging question held me back. If both the future and the past were within my reach—and I really believed they were—then why was there no record of my travels?

I found the answer while mulling things over at my favorite bar. An emergency news broadcast cut in on the TV, interrupting the game. The image on the screen showed an I.C.B.M. streaking toward the city.

all time within reach
no time for hesitation
untimely demise

Robot Baldur
Denise Noe

ARTICLES

HEADLINES AND BULLWHIPS
Robert E. Porter

A-1, B-2...
C-3 P ode!
The translation of one language into another is not as simple as a child's substitution code. It requires creativity and a Janus-like cultural understanding on the part of the translator. Can he tailor the original to fit a new empirical context? When in Rome, the fig leaf must become a toga, etc.

Kenneth Rexroth translated a haiku by Toshiyuki as a two-liner:

Autumn has come invisibly.
Only the wind's voice is ominous.
(Rexroth)

There are seventeen syllables.
Why?
Why not?
Should we read Alexander Pope's verse or TE Lawrence's prose translation of Homer? Should we define poetry by rhythm alone, or by the rhythmic compression and decompression of meaning? Much humor and truth can be derived by shifting from the specific to the general, or vice Versace.

There are no right answers.
So, what's left?
Good questions!
A translator makes choices over the course of his translation. To achieve some effects, others must be compromised. The result is not an

approximation of the original. It is one of many arguments for how best to represent the original now -- in *this* language, for *this* audience.

Should we fall for the fallacies of a Popist gunpowder plotter or a Lawrencian dynamite-throwing partisan?

No!

There can be strength in the diversity of translations if they argue well, with respect for their differences.

Left- and right-wingers fly around in their own respective circles. They'll never get very far. They have ignored the best counsel at Delphi: Nothing too much! They swallowed the predigested *vermis et vomitus* brought up by the sweaty sock puppet at the end of some Lovecraftian thing's propaganda arm. Better to have balance in our lives, and in our literary diets. To fly over the moon, both wings need to work together.

In his 1953 textbook for the University of Wisconsin, Bruce Westley showed a watchdog journalist's ideal. What is balance and moderation? Accuracy over sensationalism. For ex.,

> There is nothing like unanimity in the use of the hyphen. But its presence or absence can make a lot of difference in a headline. Note its effect in this headline:
>
> **Sheep Killing Dogs
> in Roberts County**
>
> *Now that's interesting. It's usually the other way around. And so it was in this story. The head writer meant:*

**Sheep-Killing Dogs
In Roberts County**
(Westley)

Can you imagine a third line for that first headline, to fit the more (inaccurate) sensational demands of horror ku? For ex.,

*Sheep Killing Dogs
in Roberts County--
Wool over a shepherd's eyes*

And consider this more recent CNN headline:
**New US dietary guidelines
Including babies and toddlers
For first time**
(Strickland)

Could the association with Swift's "Modest Proposal" be unintentional? I don't know. But their poor choice of words (in the context of a conspiracy theorist's fake news binge) has given us a readymade horror ku.

Westley presented another troublesome headline:

**Dartmouth man feigns
Intelligence in Germany**

Saying,

Head writers capitalize on well-established frames of reference common to a majority of newspaper readers. That helps tell some stories – but the editor cannot overlook the prospect that such common frames of reference will also convey unintended meanings.

(Westley)

I doubt Dartmouth's known for intellectual frauds. But Westley wrote this during the McCarthy era, when know-nothing lynch mobs drove Russian fluency and other much-needed expertise out of the state department, AEC, the military, etc. So, they left the Free World more vulnerable to real spies like Kim Philby, Guy Burgess, and Donald MacLean. Americans also gushed over James Bond. How could anyone so conspicuous be effective in intelligence? Might as well try to tail someone while driving a red Ferrari. Or sneak into the Oval Office wearing a Hollywood ninja outfit.

But... Who wants truth in fiction? Especially science fiction? So, why not touch up that headline:

> *Dartmouth "man"*
> *feigns intelligence*
> *in Germany*

We might up the science fictional quotient in rewrites. Dartmouth's "conscious" automaton feeds the Abwehr (or Stasi) misinformation? German "intelligence" falls for a Zoltar fortune-telling machine? Wasting their nation's resources and manpower – like those titular *Men Who Stared at Goats*? Extrapolating from there, we'd come to a surprise ending to WWII or the Cold War. That "Aha!" moment so characteristic of O. Henry, the whodunit, or haiku.

In his introduction to *One-hundred from the Japanese*, Kenneth Rexroth said:

"The kake kotoba or pivot word is a word or part of a word employed in two senses, or, very rarely, in three, one relating to what precedes, the other to what follows." And: "The pivot word shades into the pun, and some Japanese poems have so many puns that they may have two or more quite dissimilar meanings." (Rexroth)

SF and mystery writer Fredric Brown was famous for his puns and plot twists. He was a minimalist, too; some of his stories run less than a page. For years, he made a living as a Milwaukee newspaper's proof-reader and type-setter. Westley mentioned this paper (*The Milwaukee Journal*) in his acknowledgements. Did the two know each other? They might have. I heard that Brown had a regular column in the trade journals. His work typified a journalist's approach to language and wordplay with regard to world events. He took nothing too seriously. Man bites dog –as a shaggy dog story?   That could explain everything!

And show us the way...

To pare a big science fictional idea down to its essence. To quit wasting time and begin writing more effective scifaiku, something to grab your audience like the best newspaper headline – with a bullwhip's supersonic wisecrack. Why, that belongs in a museum!

Harry Harrison Ford Museum's
Soylent Greenfield Village People

WORKS CITED

Rexroth, Kenneth. *One Hundred Poems from the Japanese*, New Directions: New York, 1964.

Strickland, Ashley and Andrea Diaz and Sandee LaMotte. "New US Dietary Guidelines Include Babies and Toddlers for First Time." CNN, 30 Dec 2020.

Westley, Bruce. *News Editing*. Houghton Mifflin, 1953.

Kimo: Word Pictures
Herb Kauderer

The kimo is modelled on the haiku, but diverges in a number of ways. First, its syllable counts for each of three lines are 10/7/6. Second, enjambment is much more common. In fact, I have seen words split across lines to satisfy syllable counts making the poem as much 23 syllables broken into three lines as a poem built up of lines of set syllable counts.

Third, while haiku can be linked together, it's usually preferred that they stand alone as well. They are linked poems. The kimo is just as much a stanza format as a poetic form of its own. While the kimo appear to be just six syllables longer than a haiku, they are effectively longer than that, as kimo often have titles and haiku usually do not.

The kimo is an Israeli verse form arising from the cultural explosion that followed the formation of Israel in 1948. Many speculate that Hebrew really wanted more syllables for the minimalist form, so the extra syllables and the addition of a title addressed this need.

A haiku wants image and reflection, with a cutting word which implies action. One of the guidelines of kimo is no movement, at least in each stanza though moving from stanza to stanza can create motion. Each kimo should be a word picture. Of course a number of them strung together can give the illusion of movement just as riffling through photos can. Here is a simple word photo style kimo:

anticipations

the fireplace crackles gleeful & bright
beckoning carpet in front
so far remains empty

And here is an example of kimo as stanza format:

the weather outside

a May snow falls on the budding tulips
dust on brightly splashed petals
melting, to paint plants wet

in the house, faces pressed against window
children hope to play in snow
mother prays for flowers

For the SpecPo community, the hope is that this form can adapt to the genre. The no movement clause is a more difficult restriction to SF/F/H than other restrictions from other verse forms, particularly as minimalist SpecPo places value on aha moments, which are harder to achieve in a still photo. For example, does the following kimo violate 'no movement?'

the rhythms of home

flying saucer spins in tune with homeworld
sensor probe orbits like luna
paces menstruation

The saucer spins, though without exterior markings this might not be obvious in a photo. On the other hand, the orbiting sensor probe is clearly moving. That it is in a repetitive pattern cannot be interpreted as it being inert. In art classes and photography classes, the capturing of movement into a still graphic is considered a good thing. How does that apply to the speculative kimo? Should it look more like a still life? Or something in an SF convention art show?

The previous poem shows movement, so perhaps it doesn't qualify. The next sample implies movement, but doesn't show it. Perhaps it does qualify.

secret rendezvous

in the airducts of the space colony
the chittering of vermin
Katie sees her pet's face

There is a movement of sound, but no physical movement need be represented in the graphic that's been captured. I can draw this easily enough (or more likely my youngest daughter could, as she's the family artist these days). In some cases the image persists over time, which is a thing captured in stills better than in motion, but the requirement of 'no movement' still raises questions. I argue that the following is the essence of non-movement even if the initial image is of a rocket traveling fifty five kilometers per second.

the long game

rocket orbits star patiently waiting
for rocky planets to form
and new life to evolve

Sometimes words paint photos that painters would have a hard time realizing. It seems fair to ask then if these are actual word photos. An example follows:

meeting the neighbors

a culture descended from arachnids
the humans stumble over
number system base eight

A graphic artist would have to interpret this into a scene evolved from the poem. But simply illustrating the poem without adaptation is impossible. Adapting a verse form to SpecPo shouldn't just apply the form to speculative ideals and tropes. Changes should be welcome if they enhance any form new to SpecPo. Clearly the highly popular scifaiku has largely ignored the requested seasonal reference of the haiku, and instead added the desire for an aha moment at the end. In this same sense of willingness to adjust, I suggest the following parameters for the kimo fom:

- three lines

- preferred but not demanded 10/7/6 syllable count
- unrhymed
- the capturing of a single moment
  o or one moment per stanza when used as a stanza form
- a static image or reflection
  o though movement can be implied
  o especially by proximity of stanzas
- conceptual content includes image when possible

Here is a single SpecPo verse following these guidelines:

brave explorer

in the steel gleam of a robot's faceplate
reflection of a new world
humans dream to follow

And here is one gone wild:

celestial objects behaving badly

asteroids prank dwarf planets creating
backdrops for comets making
obscene silhouette shows

And here is a kimo as stanza speculative poem:

remembering the lost

space colony holds holiday vigil
remembrance day reverie
important ancestors

immortalized in hymns and photographs
fill the hallway monitors
though populace ignores

vision and hearing long ago lost to
radiation storms and failed shields
computers don't speak braille

Like scifaiku, rengay, and other forms, kimo also
lends itself to collaboration or playful competition
with poets alternating stanzas.

    machines know flowers
        Herb Kauderer, David Clink, Halli Villegas

|

in darkling forest on darker planet
infrared rover plunders
local magical herbs

on a bright and distant magical plain
a man awaits the rover
its supplies much needed

the roots of the herbs go deep down to the
core twined around the heart of
this night-washed lonely star

planets are bound, by science and magic
by starlight and dark woodland
by machines and flowers

In the end, the specpo kimo is what we make of it. These are my suggestions and examples. I look forward to reading what others contribute to the form.

FEATURED POET:
Tyler McIntosh

alley moonlight
in a pale hand
dreamvial

jacking in
for the concert
a deaf man's cheer

reflection
in the starship hull
granddad's eyes

meditation pill
the slowness
of melting

memory vault
even the thickest steel
warps

taxi pod
blinks confirmation
final goodbyes

after-hours
her neon eyes
in time to the beat

abandoned hospital
the flicker
of an EEG

shedding
another circuit
dry slither

a gas-masked child
awaits the bus
butterfly holo

summer night
we lay to count
security drones

robin eggs
a beak cracks
the plastic

doodles in the snow
a dealer and his baggie
of brain chips

hunting season
the wide eyes
of a telepath

icicles
on the cryotank
rosebud dawn

the rusted joint
of a timber bot
fallen maple leaves

stimsuit
developer bug
paralysis

pulsing membrane
a chaperone ushers us
away from the womb

grieving
in a world gone fast
session timeout

twin moons rising
a lone figure
with two shadows

spacesuit rack
every name tag
the same

babel fish
forgiveness
at the cemetery

butter paddle
on the ansible
a red leaf falling

lunar gala
the float of heels
thin as breath

aspen gold
their wires
entwine

another of me
behind bars
asking why

adjusting our orbit
just enough
first freeze

first weeds
fill the cracks
lunar transitway

full moon
the bare curve
of her shortening jaw

BIOGRAPHY OF FEATURED POET Tyler McIntosh

Tyler McIntosh is an environmental scientist based out of Colorado, where he loves to explore and experience the natural landscape. His academic work focuses on complex social-ecological systems such as deforestation and wildfire regimes in the context of global ecological change. *His haiku and work in related forms have appeared in numerous print and online journals such as Modern Haiku, The Heron's Nest, Frogpond, Bottle Rockets, Prune Juice, Hedgerow, Drifting Sands,* and *Contemporary Haibun Online,* among others. His work has been nominated for both the Touchstone Haiku and Haibun awards and included in anthologies such as Haiku 2021 by *Modern Haiku Press, bird whistle* by *Bottle Rockets Press,* and the 2022 and 2023 *Dwarf Stars* collections from the Science Fiction & Fantasy Poetry Association.

INTERVIEW WITH FEATURED POET **Tyler McIntosh**

How long have you been writing poetry?

I've enjoyed writing poetry ever since I was a child and vividly remember learning about haiku in elementary school. I wrote casually through college, but never considered the fact that I could submit my work for publication. It wasn't until I had my first work accepted to Scifaikuest at the end of 2020 (thanks, Teri!!) that I realized that there was space for me in the world of published poets. Since that time I've focused my work on ku-related forms, most recently branching out to experiment with haibun.

Did you begin writing haiku before you branched out to scifaiku?

I first started writing haiku (not counting my elementary school creations) as a way to cope with a concussion that I had in 2019. At a time when I was unable to look at a screen or page for very long, haiku provided me with a way to write in short bursts, and in a way that honored the more meditative and observational state of being that I was forced to embrace as a result of my injury. This style of writing naturally evolved to include scifaiku.

How did you learn about scifaiku?

I have always loved fantasy, science fiction, and all things speculative. It was only natural to eventually bring these genres to my work in short form poetry, and, out of curiosity, to subsequently look up whether there were forms and outlets dedicated to this type of writing.

Where did you learn to write scifaiku?

My first scifaiku were written without having read any other scifaiku and before I knew that such a genre existed. I tried to bring the same elegance and space for the reader to the speculative as I did ordinary haiku. This remains my ever-so-close and yet ever-so-distant goal.

Do you write poetry other than genre poetry? If so, what kind?

I write lyric free verse poetry in addition to my work in Japanese forms such as haiku, senryu, and haibun. Lyric free verse poetry provides me with a more open form in which to express myself, and often evolves from journaling or free writing. In general, fixed forms frustrate me, meaning that I very much appreciate modern English language haiku and its departure from a prescribed 5-7-5 form.

Whose poetry has influenced you the most?

There are many poets (and other writers!) whose work has greatly influenced me; I try to read widely. One particular poet whom I am indebted to is **Mike Rehling,** *the founder of* 'Failed Haiku - A Journal of English Senryu.' *Mike took me under his wing when I first began publishing in the world of haiku and senryu, reviewed and improved my work, and helped me learn the ins-and-outs of submitting work to publish. Thanks, Mike!*

Who is your favorite poet?

I struggle with favorites; I find that the work of many poets strikes a chord within me at different times depending on my state of mind. However, long-form poets that I consistently come back to are **Li-Young Lee** *and* **Mary Oliver.** *In the world of ku I always admire the work of* **Peter Newton, Lee Gurga,** *and* **Roberta Beary.**

What/who is your main inspiration?

As is the case for many haiku poets, I have a close relationship to the natural world. I developed this relationship through my childhood in Wyoming, and it informs my professional academic work as well as my writing. My father, who passed away a few years ago, played an essential role in fostering this relationship; his fingerprints can be found throughout my work. When writing scifaiku, I find myself trying to capture the 'haiku/senryu moments' of the future, as well as drawing from fairy tales, mythology, and the work of many exceptional science fiction writers and artists who have come before me.

What poetry magazines do you read/contribute to?

I read and contribute to many journals across the world, and admire many of them. I hold particular admiration for Acorn, The Heron's Nest, Kingfisher, *and* Hedgerow, *as well as the haibun-focused outlets* Drifting Sands *and* Contemporary Haibun.

MY FAVORITE POEM by editor, **t.santitoro**

As Tyler McIntosh says in his interview above, "I struggle with favorites". So well said! Indeed, in this issue, I too struggle with finding a favorite. I think choosing a particular poem means finding one that "speaks" to me. Well, the following poems all spoke very loudly:

MMO

lonely avatar
knight stands eternally still
his Player grew old

H.T. Grossen

What a poignant and sad scifaiku! It's like watching Andy grow up and leave his toys behind in the Toy Story movies!

little robot
vacuum cleaner
my toes are not snacks

N.E. Taylor

And this poem is equally as funny and cute as the previous one was sad! An up-lifting ku!

i know the names
of ghosts
old answering machine

N.E. Taylor

Who doesn't know the grief of listening, on an old answering machine recording, to the voice of a loved one who has passed?

In Hungry Times

when the famine doesn't end
Mother's desperate hands reveal
you're not the favorite child

-**H.V. Patterson**

OH YIKES! This horrorku should have been sent to Tales of the Moonlit Path's Demented Mother's Day issue!!! Wow! That last line is killer!!!

home alone
by **Denise Noe**

home
alone
for a century
for a thousand years
rub oh! rub sweet human
set me free
this genie

And, finally, a thoughtful poem about a lonely genie! I never actually thought about them being "home alone". Wow.

Well, there you have it. All the poems which especially touched my soul. Which ones touched YOURS?

www.ingramcontent.com/pod-product-compliance
Lightning Source LLC
LaVergne TN
LVHW092058060526
838201LV00047B/1459